SOVEREIGN REIN

by **SCOTT KNUDSEN**

LEADERSHIP
Thoughtful, Relevant Leaders From Around The World
BOOKS

Most Leadership Books products are available at special quantity discounts for bulk purchases for sales promotions, premiums, fund-raising and educational needs. For details, visit our website at www.leadershipbooks.com

Sovereign Rein
By: Scott Knudsen
Copyright: 2023
Publisher: Leadership Books, Inc.
Las Vegas, Nevada & New York, NY

LeadershipBooks.com

For Worldwide Distribution

International Standard Book Number:
Hardcover: 978-1-951648-63-3
Paperback: 978-1-951648-64-0
eBook: 978-1-951648-65-7

Printed in the United States of America

LEADERSHIP
Thoughtful, Relevant Leaders From Around The World
BOOKS

ACKNOWLEDGMENT

I would like to thank my beautiful wife, Tracy, and our incredible daughter Hailey for always being there for me. I want to thank the medical teams that have worked and fixed me back up so I can get back to doing what I love- being a cowboy. I would like to thank Leadership Books for helping guide me with this book so I can share stories of the Western way of life. Most importantly, I thank my Lord and Savior, Jesus Christ -I love writing about everything He has done in my life. And thank you - the reader for taking the time to read my stories.

TABLE OF CONTENTS

FOREWORD

Jerry "Gerardo" Diaz, Charro de Corazon, world-renowned horseman, and rope artist, embodies the cultural tradition of his family as a 4th generation Champion Charro. His company, Jerry Diaz Productions, highlights his family's horsemanship talents and his amazing roping skills in Rodeos and Mexican Extravaganzas that he produces. Presenting his Charro Production horsemanship mastery at the Olympics in 1996 in Atlanta and at the World Economic Summit in Houston for seven world leaders, including George and Barbara Bush and Margaret Thatcher, demonstrated his Charro Heritage to the world.

As a lifetime member and director of major stock shows and rodeos, Jerry and his famous horses were voted PRCA Rodeo Act of the Year. Keeping the Charro tradition alive, he has been inducted into the Texas Cowboy Hall of Fame, the Cowboys of Color Museum, and the Hall of Fame, and he has a star on the Texas Trail of Fame at the

Fort Worth, Texas, Stockyards. The Federation of Charros has bestowed him with their prestigious Golden Spur Award. Believing in God and family tradition, Jerry's dedication to the Heritage of the Charro and living the Western lifestyle on his Texas ranch with his beautiful wife, Staci, son Nicolas and their talented horses endears him to his fans worldwide.

Jerry and Scott met in 2019 when, coincidentally, they were seated next to each other on a plane after a VIP Purina World Tour in St. Louis, Missouri. As the conversation between "The Charro" and "The Cowboy" ensued, they soon discovered that they are brothers in the Christian faith and had similar family ranching traditions and a special love of roping. Scott's daughter, Hailey, and Jerry's son, Nicolas, were at the forefront of the discussion, each one wanting to follow their dad's cowboy culture and Charro lifestyle as part of their future careers. Finding so much common ground, Jerry and Scott became fast friends. With all of this in mind, Jerry wholeheartedly recommends Scott's newest book, Sovereign Rein, with seventeen stories and authentic photos of true cowboy life that relate back to verses from the Bible, friendships formed, and cowboy events encountered.

SOVEREIGN REIN

Middle English: from Old French sovereign,
based on Latin super 'above'.

sov·er·eign

1. Having supreme rank or power: a sovereign prince.

2. Paramount; supreme: Her sovereign virtue
is compassion.

CHAPTER 1

LIGHTNING OUT OF THE BLUE

It was a beautiful summer day and not a cloud in the sky. A storm seemed to be approaching from the East, but it was far off – approximately eighteen miles. Today was going to be a fun day because it was Hailey's first birthday. As first-time parents, we had many activities planned. Tracy and daughter Hailey were waiting down at the barn for me, so I drove down to the barn. Getting out of my truck, Tracy handed me our one-year-old baby girl, Hailey.

I remember this day as if it were yesterday. I was holding Hailey in my left arm, and Tracy was standing to my right. Out of the clear blue sky came the loudest noise and the brightest light we have ever seen. It was a bolt from the blue -a lightning strike.

The bolt struck the top of my head, went through my body, down my left arm, and exited my body out of the hand which held Hailey.

I collapsed to the ground.

My first thoughts were, "Is Hailey okay? Is Tracy okay? What just happened?" Thankfully, I see Tracy holding Hailey, and they were both looking at me, "Are **you** okay?"

As my mind tried to process what occurred, I felt an intense burning on the top of my head and on my hand. I saw horses running around and into each other. I heard the chickens making the craziest of noises and saw them trying to fly. One hundred and fifty yards away, in the backyard, the water pipes were coming out of the ground. Three hundred yards away, irrigation lines popped out of the ground. None of this made any sense.

Tracy and I looked at each other in disbelief. Our minds could not comprehend what our eyes were seeing. At first, it seemed like someone played a joke on us. Could we have been hit by lightning on a sunny day? It was like in the 50s when you would unplug the TV to plug it back into the wall and all the funny lines would appear. That was what it felt like in our heads. It was mental. It's like the saying you've always heard –when you least expect it, you might be struck by lightning. We never really think it will happen to us, but it can. I had been struck by a bolt from the blue while holding my infant daughter, Hailey.

I got up, dusted myself off, shook off the blow, and somehow, we made it up to the house. The shock of it all, coupled with the excitement of Hailey's party, made us believe we were ok. Thankful that we were okay, Tracy and I continued on with Hailey's birthday plans -Tracy went to town, thirty minutes away, to get the birthday cake for the big party. Neither of us realized how bad she or I was.

Tracy arrived home to find me deliriously attempting to call the hospital on the keypad of the desktop computer. The top half of my face was black, and the underneath of my eyes was black also. The shock of the bolt had worn off by now, and decided it was time to go to the Emergency Room.

The ER docs treated me, Tracy and Hailey. Tracy and Hailey had minor injuries, but the lightning strike caused me some serious internal damage, memory loss, and other negative things.

Over the next few years, I had to learn to read, write, and drive my truck all over again. Months later, as I was sitting on the couch eating popcorn and my fillings fell out. It took me years to recover. I was to treat my head injury like a concussion, as the doctors had not seen a survivor of a lightning strike before. So many people were praying for us and helping our family with all the ranch chores.

Tracy's decision to take me to the hospital saved my life. My injuries were extensive but miraculously minor in comparison to what they could have been. Tracy's and Hailey's were almost non-existent, Thank God. Not many people survive a lightning strike, but we did.

Through the quick thinking of the doctors and medical staff, and the many prayers received by our family and friends, we recovered quickly, and Hailey had her first birthday party right on schedule- as if that bolt from the blue never happened.

I took this time to be with my family, and I was blessed to have it. Now the family is doing great! We are aware of the storms and even the ones that are not close to us.

PSALMS 68:20 —OUR GOD IS A GOD WHO SAVES! THE SOVEREIGN LORD RESCUES US FROM DEATH.

CHAPTER 2

DIABLO

I kept hearing about this beautiful horse that has been going from trainer to trainer. He just would not hook up with any trainer. So, of course, I wanted an opportunity to work with him, being such a difficult case. I talked to different people who tried every method and creative idea with this horse, but that had yet to work.

This horse was a big bay gelding who was unusually athletic, really fast, and very smart. He had so much potential to be one of the best ranch horses I could've ever had. So, we get him on the ranch and start working with him. Right away, I could tell by the cold body language, the tense muscles, the posture of his head, and the twitching of his tail that this was going to be "the ultimate challenge."

We continued working together –me asking him, but him not giving in. But I was confident that, given the chance, he would eventually do the right thing. I was wrong. We worked together a lot, very soft yet proven methods of horsemanship –he didn't care.

I got a saddle on him and eventually put one foot in a stirrup and swung my right leg over his back end to get situated in the saddle. We worked together pretty well, but only for a short amount of time. Then he went to running really fast, then straight to bucking and not a stride-it-out rocking-chair type of bucking, but a very violent and incredibly hard professional type of bucking.

I was using every method I could to slow him down, and then the one thing I remembered to stop him from bucking was to go forward and use the forward momentum as a deterrent to his bucking of going up and down and sideways. As I asked him and pressed him to go forward, he stopped, planted all four of his big hooves into the sand, and jumped up and backward. The apex of the fall was my neck, then my body in the saddle, and then an eleven-hundred-pound horse. That was it.

I don't remember anything when I finally did come to. I didn't know where I was or how long I'd been gone. All I can remember is my hands trying to grab something, and it was the cold sand going through my fingers, just like an hourglass. I couldn't move - I was gone.

I do remember seeing him, not vividly, almost like a cloud looking at me with those cold brown eyes. I don't know how long I was there. Eventually, I could move, but I knew I was knocked out cold for a period of time.

I knew had I hurt my neck and had a concussion. I didn't realize how bad I ended up. I ended up breaking my neck. We made it to the hospital, and after some incredible surgery, many great doctors and medical teams worked to put the plates in and get me healed up.

I did end up riding that horse, but it wasn't for some time later. I wanted to be the one to finish the story –not him. The bay gelding's name was Diablo. He earned it.

DEUTERONOMY 30:15 "NOW LISTEN! TODAY I AM GIVING YOU A CHOICE BETWEEN LIFE AND DEATH, BETWEEN PROSPERITY AND DISASTER.

CHAPTER 3

DRINK WATER AND STAY HEALTHY

I have always tried to stay in shape. I love working out. I feel that eating right and taking care of my body makes me a better cowboy and a rancher. My body is working and used so hard every day I have to stay fit. When you are a horseman, you must keep in sync with your horse, so it is super important to be physically fit, limber, and in tune with your horse.

I was working out really hard every day, and I would carry a plastic water jug, one gallon, so I would drink water throughout the day to stay hydrated, take care of my muscles, and do all I knew I needed to do. After a few weeks, I noticed I started losing muscle mass and lots of weight, and my energy started dropping. Finally, I became sick. I did what I always do and thought I could just work through it, overcome it, and be better because of it. This wasn't the case.

I remember walking near the edge of my bed one day, getting ready for work. The sun was not up, and I fell down. My wife Tracy heard it, and she asked what fell, and I had to tell her it was me. I had lost so much weight –almost as much as a feed sack, that's fifty pounds. Tracy rushed me to the hospital, which we were very familiar with.

When we went inside, they immediately stopped helping everyone and directed their focus toward me. I did not like that. They immediately rolled me back to the red room, which is the most serious unit. Tracy went back there with me, and I remember the look in their eyes, the nervousness, and the frantic pace they worked at as I lay there.

Tracy had not had anything to eat since the day before, around lunch, so after almost twenty-four hours, she asked the nurse if she could go get a sandwich, and the nurse said, "You stay by his side for as long as you can. I will get you something to eat." Tracy looked at me, and I couldn't turn to look at her, much less focus. I hated that!

We have been in the ER a lot with my occupation, and we've always been able to leave, so we expected to leave and go home that afternoon to take care of our animals and go on with our life. The doctors and nurses said it will probably be a week if we're lucky and he gets to leave. Those first few days were really tough, not that I remember a lot, but I was definitely in another place. That is a story and a book for another time.

After many days in the hospital, I was released. It took months to get back to almost normal. Once we figured out what happened –thank goodness for great doctors and the lab technician's hard work, we eventually figured out I got so sick because of the plastic water bottle. Even though I cleaned the water bottle every night, I didn't clean it with bleach, and when using plastic, it needs to have bleach to kill all the germs.

What happened was this: I left out that one small detail by trying to take care of myself, I gave myself E. coli (Escherichia coli), Salmonella and C. diff (Clostridioides difficile).

With lots of prayers, visits, and well wishes from my family, friends, and the community, I was able to heal up and get back to riding. As in the book of

James, the prayers of healing offered in faith will heal the sick.

JAMES 5:16 "THE EFFECTIVE, FERVENT PRAYER OF A RIGHTEOUS MAN AVAILS MUCH,"

CHAPTER 4

THE PASTURE IS MY STAGE

I used to ride and train horses for a very well-known person in the entertainment world. I loved it; he was such a great man and loved the Western lifestyle. At one of his ranches, they took off a bunch of cattle, all but three. He called me saying he couldn't get these three and asked if I could do it. Instantly I said yes, as I couldn't wait for the opportunity, and I hooked up the trailer, grabbed one of my best horses, and headed out.

This place was a pretty good size –a couple of thousand acres, and the cows were worked into a five-hundred-acre trap. When I got out there, I found out they had never been around a horse or human and didn't really want to be. I was able to get one caught, although the other two I couldn't, but not from the lack of trying.

As I was driving out of that ranch, I was thinking about how I was going to catch those other two cows, and I knew I needed some help. So, I called two great cowboys –my dad and brother. I asked if they would come up the next day, I would have the horses, and we would get to the cowboy. I knew my sister and mom couldn't help as they already had plans, but they could absolutely ride as well. At the same time, I had a writer from Baltimore, Maryland shadowing me, writing some cowboy stories and poetry.

So, the next morning we all go to the ranch. It is me, my dad and brother, the writer from Baltimore with his family, and the owner of the ranch with his entourage. So, we had roughly forty people watching the action in the pasture as they sat around in their trucks and cars.

No pressure?

The three of us had to stay calm for the horses and the two cows we had left. These cattle weren't your normal cattle. They would charge us because they could jump over a six-foot fence and whatever else they wanted to do. We call these types of cattle "waspy cattle" on account of the way they dart around.

We had three of my best ranch horses. At one point, the waspy cattle had my hat, my brother's hat, and my dad's hat while we were in another pasture, and that goes against every cowboy code there is! They both were so aggressive.

We did go in and get our hats that the brush and wind knocked off. The hats were probably loosened a bit by those heifers too! We got one cow caught, put her in the pen, and then moved into the trailer. The second one was another story.

At one point, I turned around, and she lifted my dad and my good gelding on top of the cedar bush. She pushed my brother into some cactus, and then she headed my way and lifted me and my eleven-hundred-pound gelding off the ground. We did end up getting her caught even though she jumped out twice. The third time we finally got her loaded in the trailer and off to the auction barn. Thank goodness they have eight-foot fences!

PROVERBS 16:3 "COMMIT YOUR ACTIONS TO THE LORD, AND YOUR PLANS WILL SUCCEED."

CHAPTER 5

INVERTED OREO

I was busy working with a lot of new horses at the ranch over the weekend. Many were young. It was a Friday, and I had Saturday and Sunday to assess this group of horses to see what we had. I had to leave the following Monday morning at 6 a.m. and go north to Dallas, Texas, for a three-day meeting. I am not one to cancel meetings or be late because I am always respectful of someone else's time, so this had to be done by Sunday night.

Saturday and most of Sunday went well, but I had one more horse to ride that Sunday afternoon. It was a beautiful sorrel gelding, and I was riding him very well. I quickly found out (as I was riding him and doing roping and doing basic maneuvers that I had used on several previous horses) that this gelding was different. He got spooked and began to buck.

As this guy was bucking me, he turned to his right and went right into the rope. That was dangerous, but he kept doing it. Usually, I can stop that, but this time I couldn't because my right hand was underneath the rope, caught in between the saddle on the bottom and the rope on the top, so I was getting corkscrewed on top of the horse with a rope going around me, tightening –an absolutely terrible situation.

After what seemed like forever, but it probably was only a minute or two, I was able to get the horse to slow down and calm down by calming myself down —if you are calm and relaxed, the horse will also calm and relax. I then brushed him with my left hand, and once he relaxed, I was safely able to move the rope and free my right hand. Once we were all untangled and calm, I got off the horse –well, really fell off the horse. He was fine, but I wasn't.

Once I regained my breath, I made sure the horse was fine, got back on him, finished our ride on the saddle and made it to the house. That's when I knew lots of things were wrong. When I looked at myself in the mirror, I looked like an inverted Oreo from my chest to my knees was black and blue. I knew I hurt myself really bad but thank goodness the horse was perfect.

I went to bed Sunday night with ice packed all over me, and the next morning I was up at four in the morning feeding horses and then off on my way to Dallas, which is a five-hour drive. I made it to Dallas, checked into the hotel, and then dashed to a large drugstore. I bought huge bandages, regular bandages, wraps, band-aids, creams, and antiseptic for all the cuts, including a couple of fingers and a half-arm brace. Then I went back to the hotel and doctored myself. But I made the meetings that Monday morning!

The meetings went all day, so there was no way I could see a doctor. So, I called somebody in my hometown, and we set up an appointment for late Friday afternoon when I would be back home. I rolled into the doctor's office just in time for my appointment, and the doctor who had worked on me many times already said, "You Cowboys are really something! You tolerate pain, doctor yourselves, and laugh when you tell the story!"

He's right! After an hour or so in his office, we realized I had a couple of cracked ribs, a bruised sternum, a fractured left arm, and multiple bruises between my knees and my sternum from the saddle horn. Soon as we got fixed up the next day, I was riding that horse yeah, the original name of the gelding was Ol' Red because he was such a beautiful deep cherry-red color.

I know that's not original, but it fits. I did heal up eventually, and Ol' Red became one of the favorites. I am so glad that the horse helped introduce me to one of my favorite surgeons.

**LUKE 5:31 JESUS ANSWERED THEM,
"HEALTHY PEOPLE DON'T NEED A DOCTOR—SICK
PEOPLE DO."**

CHAPTER 6

SAY YES

A few years ago, my niece asked me to speak at her university. At that time, people who knew me knew I didn't like to speak in public or have any attention put on me because I felt the attention should always be on the horses. She calmly and creatively said it was just for our club. Well, I always say yes to my daughter, nephews, and my niece.

I could prepare a nice talk about horses, take her out for dinner, and then go back home to the hill country of Texas. However, that wasn't the case, as her club had just won the national championship. So, the room was full of students, professors, administrators, and friends. The school was Texas A&M University. There was no way I was going to waltz in and out of Texas A&M. Not at this celebrated dinner! My goodness, what did I say yes to?

I thought I had a good talk prepared. I focused on the back wall behind everyone as I spoke. My plan was mainly to talk about horses to make me comfortable. Well, I did my talk and then said they could ask any questions if they wanted.

The first question was, "Have you ever been hurt?" Now, there is a Cowboy code that you never talk about your injuries, but I had to because I said I would. The second question, "Have you ever failed?" These are two questions that I've never spoken about publicly, but I did that night, and I was surprised to notice how the room became smaller. We all leaned in. We had a great night.

The club helped me as much as I hopefully helped them. After the talk, I met all the students, and I listened to what these incredible students had to say about why they'd come to Texas A&M and what they hoped to achieve. After listening to them, I truly believe they will achieve everything they told me that night.

The next day we were given a tour of Texas A&M, and it was so much fun. The hospitality was Texas size. I will never forget those two days; and thank goodness I said yes.

MATHEW 10:20 "OR IT IS NOT YOU WHO WILL BE SPEAKING-IT
WILL BE THE SPIRIT OF YOUR
FATHER SPEAKING THROUGH YOU."

CHAPTER 7

NOBODY YELL FIRE

had a major neck injury working a horse, well I broke it- my neck. We ended up going to a fantastic San Antonio, Texas hospital. It was state of the art, Dr. owned, and 100 percent focused on the patients and their families. My neck injury was so bad that they had to operate -I did not know they would belt you into bed after neck surgery.

Well, that's exactly what happened; the medical staff strapped down each leg, my arms, and my waist. I was also in a neck brace. I understood why they did this because any movement would have messed up the surgery. I was grateful for the extra care and protection they provided me, but it was mentally and physically uncomfortable.

As you read the stories, I'm sure you realize my wife and daughter are in a lot of hospital rooms but thank goodness it's for me and not them.

This particular night, my wife was looking out the window of the San Antonio skyline while I was strapped in bed, unable to move. She turned her head away from the window and looked at me. I could tell by her expression that something was wrong.

At first, I thought she saw the numbers over my head on the monitors. That wasn't it at all. Then we heard sirens and more and more sirens, and they got louder as if they were coming closer. As the sirens made these loud noises, I saw red and blue reflections on the window. By the way, Tracy was looking out the window, I could tell she was looking at something, but she didn't want to say to me yet. Finally, I had the courage to ask her. She told me fire trucks were coming to the hospital.

At that moment, all at once, I could hear the doors down the hospital hallway slamming shut. I was up on one of the top floors, and as my wife looked down at the fire trucks, she could see that the hospital sign and part of the building were on fire. I have really put myself in some pretty tough positions, but nothing like being tied down to a bed in a room on the top floor of a hospital while the hospital building was on fire. That's a whole 'nother level of nervousness which I wouldn't let show for my wife, and she wouldn't let show for me.

People came into the room saying the situation was being handled and reassuring us that the fire was being put out. The San Antonio Fire Department was able to get the fire all put out before they had to start evacuating rooms; thank goodness for that wonderful fire department.

I was released in a couple of days and got back to my house at the ranch. It was such a great feeling driving in through the front gate, and it was so hard to believe after what we had just gone through. It's so hard to describe the feeling of being tied down in bed when there's a fire several stories below. Yeah, but then again, I can't describe how wonderful it was that night to be in my own bed at the ranch.

PSALMS 112:7 "THEY DO NOT FEAR BAD NEWS: THEY CONFIDENTLY TRUST THE LORD TO TAKE CARE OF THEM."

CHAPTER 8

KEEP YOUR HEAD DOWN

I was so blessed to learn to ride a horse at a very young age. Even the day my parents brought me home from the hospital, my mom sat me on my dad's calf roping horse. He was out there and held me. This started on day one. I loved it!

When I was a very young boy - maybe ten or eleven - I had an opportunity to train a horse. My parents had quarter horses, some for ranching, and drop hands, and some for racing. My parents had one racehorse who was really well-bred. He was a big, beautiful bay (dark brown) gelding named Duroc.

Duroc was so fast out of the gate that he would be winning the race for forty, maybe fifty yards. Unfortunately, the race was 350 yards, and he could never do better than last place. One day we were in the kitchen as a family talking about his last performance, and someone asked about how he was doing in training; then someone said he ran like a Duroc. For those that don't know, a Duroc is a type of pig. No racehorse should ever be compared to a pig.

Well, knowing that he was very fast the first few yards, I thought we could turn this racehorse into a calf roping horse. Of course, in a young person's mind, it would be easy to do. After very little convincing, my parents realized that Duroc wouldn't make a racehorse, so they let my brother, sister, and I work with him. We renamed him Duroc.

I remember riding Duroc every day! It's going in a row, stopping, doing everything that a calf roping horse does. We were ready to take him to the arena to let him break out of the roping box to show how fast he was. The roping box is where the horse stands right before they release the calf. This particular roping box had a bar at the front of it several feet above the rider's head.

As a young and inexperienced trainer, there was one thing I forgot, which is that when racehorses break out of the starting gate, they launch upward and outward to get the biggest first step possible. However, a calf roping horse should launch out low so the rider can see the calf, which is a very critical step I left out of the training program.

When Duroc left the box, he went up and out. My head and the crossbar collided, knocking me off the horse and out. In a little bit, I was back on him, and we were riding around the arena enjoying the afternoon. However, that one little step I missed could've been avoided had I remembered that one difference. Nevertheless, I learned a valuable lesson –always keep your head down on your business, or it will get away from you. Ol' Duroc stayed the rest of his thirty-four years at my parent's place, helping raise kids and grandkids, and yes, he did become a pretty good roping horse.

PROVERBS 21:31 "THE HORSE IS PREPARED OF THE DAY OF BATTLE, BUT THE VICTORY BELONGS TO THE LORD."

CHAPTER 9

WHEN TEXAS FREEZES OVER

February is usually a cold month in Texas. The year was 2021, and we knew the weather would turn cold and freeze for a few days. What we didn't know was how cold or how long it would last. Living in a rural area, we know to be prepared with extra hay and grain. I would always cut, and stack bales long before winter.

We thought we were prepared for a normal Texas winter plus an extra 10 percent, just in case. When the first arctic blast hit the ranch, we knew this was not normal. The weather changed instantly. The wind was severe from out of the far north. Temperatures dropped quickly. The weather came in so fast that there was no time to prepare anymore. We had to be ready. We made sure that all the livestock was in the barn, the chickens were in the coop, the pigs and the turkeys, and that everything was where it belonged.

The first night it dropped into the teens, and the wind chill factor was in the single digits. We aren't used to that kind of weather for long periods of time. All the water for the ranch comes from a well. So, when the electricity goes off, there is no well, and when there's no well, there is no water.

If the pipes freeze, there's no water. We knew we were in trouble when the temperature wasn't getting above freezing. It was starting to become very serious with the ice and snow. We were in trouble. We have a solar-powered gate. There was so much ice on the gate and no sun that the gate wouldn't open. The electrical lines in front of the Ranch were so heavy with ice that they broke, and a line fell across our entrance. We should have been trapped. We live on a mile and a half of red granite road in the hills, twenty minutes from town. All the roads were sheeted with ice.

After the third day of single-digit windchill and freezing weather with no electricity or water, we opened the gate to go to town to get a few more supplies- taking a risk and driving over the electrical line. We made it back to the Ranch just in time for the second electrical line to fall at our entrance -no more leaving; we were trapped for good. We had animals we were responsible for and neighbors we cared for. With everything going on, neighbors kept calling each other when we had phone service, checking on each other.

After day six, we were out of water for the animals. Our local volunteer fire department stopped at the gate with some water for the animals. We ran the water hose from the fire truck around the electrical pole and into some trash cans and a hat in the back of my Kawasaki mule. I drove those down and poured them in the water in the water troughs wasn't the perfect water, but it was survival water.

On the eighth day, we were supposed to warm up to a little above freezing, so I took the snow off the ground and felt the water troughs expecting the warmth from the sun to melt the snow so we could capture it in the water troughs. But it didn't happen because another cold front blew in and froze it. We would wake up every hour and a half to check on animals and make sure they weren't in a bad spot lying down dying. We wanted to make sure they were up and moving around at least a little bit, so we were keeping the fire going because once it went out, we knew we could never get it started again.

We were starting to run out of firewood because we had never had to burn a twenty-four-hour fire for this long before. We searched for some other wood out in the pasture that was shaded with ice, and we would bring it to the front porch, where my wife would use a hammer to break the ice off; then we would bring it and put it in front of the fire to thaw it a little bit before we would put it on the fire.

We figured some heat was better than no heat. We would rope the low limbs and break them so they would not fall on the house or the barn. Walking through the pasture was so dangerous because the tree limbs were so heavy with ice that they would break and fall all on their own. It was like somebody throwing a 200-pound spear at you from twenty or thirty feet in the air.

The first couple of days, the horses got nervous and ran away from anything that they were not used to the sound of. It was so dangerous. Inside the house, it was freezing. Even the gel mattress topper was frozen. We survived sixteen days of no water and no electricity. Our animals all survived, and we survived. We did end up with frost-bite and some hyperthermia, but we survived. We did have a couple of neighbors who didn't make it and a lot of livestock around us that didn't make it. We were blessed, and somehow, we reverted to the Pioneer survival lifestyle.

JAMES 1:3 "FOR YOU KNOW WHEN YOUR FAITH IS TESTED, YOUR ENDURANCE HAS A CHANCE TO GROW."

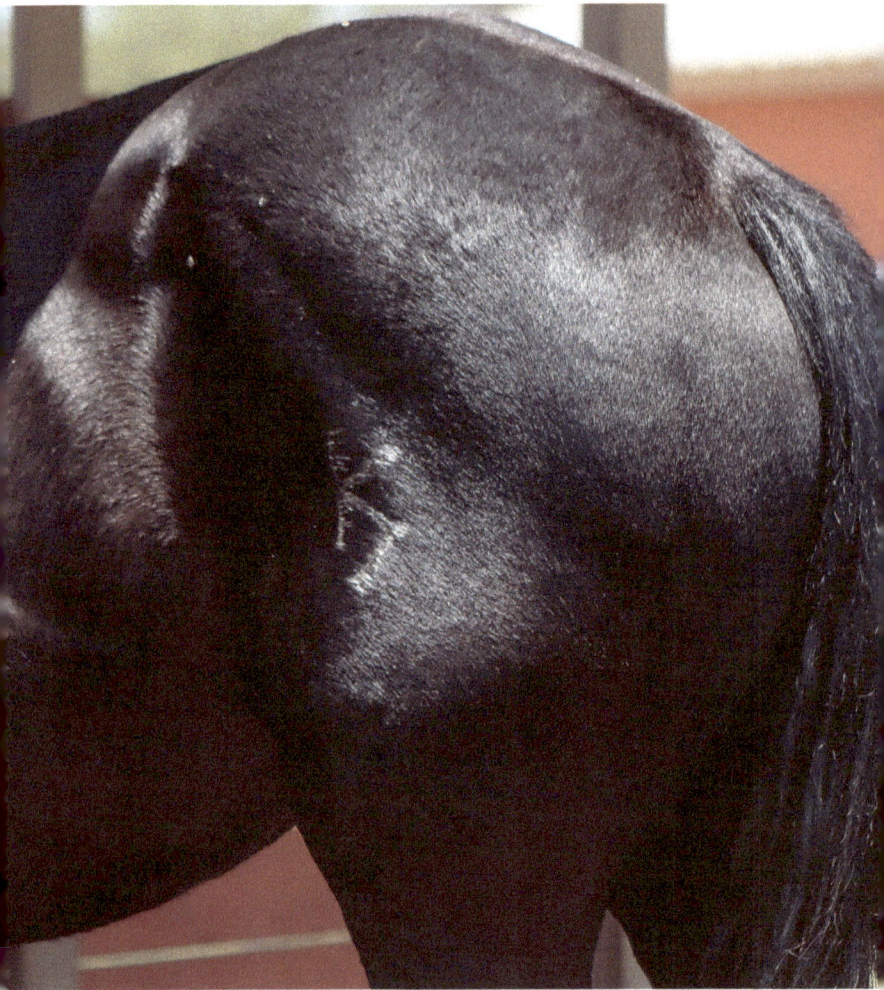

CHAPTER 10

RIDE FOR THE BRAND

As you read in the first chapter —we were hit by lightning. Being an entrepreneur and a cowboy that doesn't run away, we figured we needed to create our family brand on something our family went through. That is how we came up with the Lightning K brand.

A brand in the Western culture or mindset is so important. Corporations have a logo that helps customers identify their brand. We cowboys and ranchers create a brand that means so much more. It's what we stand for and what we believe. It shows who owns that horse and that cow. It is for protection from theft. It is a way to identify whose it is.

We take special pride in our brands. It is often handed down from generation to generation, and we want to do a good job because if we don't, people know who our family is, just as we know whom a cowboy is associated with... by the brand.

There's something very dear to me about being in agriculture, and I love being a cowboy and being in the Western industry. When we were hit by lightning, we didn't run away from being hit;, we faced it. For me, it was a great opportunity that we could share in public to encourage and inspire others.

When you have your brand on your chaps, horse, truck, trailer, even the floor of my house, like me, you take pride in it. There's a saying that goes back to the 1800s -"you ride for the brand,"–meaning "you ride- for the people" and what it stands for and for what it means to you." Heck, you'd give your life for it —if it is important enough.

After my family went through that disaster, we refused to run away because we knew we would never stop running. So, we embraced the fact that we were hit by lightning, that it caused a huge amount of physical damage to us, and while we acknowledge that, we also knew that if we grew from that horrible situation, it would make our family so much closer, and it did. It means something when we talk about riding for the brand, it truly means something. We wanted our brand to be able to tell the story, and ours sure does. It's a family story of overcoming, surviving, and re-learning.

Hopefully, the Lightning K brand can be seen by people to be helping them as an inspirational brand of what they can overcome and achieve. We sure didn't ask for that terrible accident, but we sure as heck won't run from it!

2 TIMOTHY 1:7 "FOR GOD HAS NOT GIVEN US A SPIRIT OF FEAR AND TIMIDITY BUT OF POWER, LOVE, AND SELF-DISCIPLINE."

TWO LEGS ARE BETTER THAN ONE

I grew up loving the Western way of life. I was on a horse almost daily. I would pack my saddlebags and head out early in the morning, and come home usually at dark, sometimes after.

I was riding a great quarter horse, and we were having so much fun, and I must've been around fifteen years old when one day, my horse stumbled and fell on a rock, and it hurt my left knee. We knew it was a bad blow but didn't know how bad.

It took all of us and some incredible doctors to fix my knee because it had so much damage that it was getting worse, not better. Soon I lost all the muscle in my leg. I then lost all function.

I ended up in the hospital for thirty days. The outlook didn't look good, and the doctors began to talk about amputation. But after many surgeries and lots of prayers, I could move a toe. That was so important.

My Mom would stay all day at the hospital and my Dad all night. My brother and sister helped at the house. With lots of rehabilitation therapy and positive thinking, my knee eventually became better.

I am so blessed to have a great, supporting family. I am still working out and always doing extra to make sure that my knee and leg are kept strong and taken good care of. Soon as I healed up, I was back on that horse and loving it.

**JOHN 5:8 JESUS TOLD HIM,
"STAND UP, PICK UP YOUR MAT, AND WALK."**

CHAPTER 12

HORSESHOES

I was riding colts for a lady north of town. She had the biggest, prettiest bay young gelding. He was so athletic for being so big. He was like a 6-foot-6 teenage boy –tall and lanky and kind of clumsy at times.

I was riding a flat tack saddle, and we were in a slow lope and a nice wood round pen. It was perfect; he was doing so great. He tried so hard, but he lost his balance and fell to the inside and then over-corrected to the outside, which meant my face and head smashed into the wall as he was going forward.

It spun and turned my neck, and I fell. I don't re-member a lot. I knew I had a major concussion —I've had them before and know what they feel like. The gelding was looking down at me in disbelief at what happened. The gelding and a ranch hand helped me up. It wasn't good.

The ranch hand helped me to get to the horse's water trough, and I washed my face. I knew it was damaged pretty badly. I cleaned it with the water from the trough, grabbed a handful of Texas dirt, and put it all over the right side of my face to stop the bleeding. I didn't want blood in my truck. It slowed it down, but it didn't stop it completely.

I drove the thirty minutes of back roads home. I made it! I asked my wife where the cleaning alcohol was, as I needed to doctor myself. I thought maybe I could fix it on my own. One look at me and she knew —my face around my eyes had turned black. We were headed to the hospital. Tracy, my wife, was right again.

The doctor at the emergency room said we needed surgery immediately, or I would lose my eye and part of my face. We had a great plastic surgeon to do the surgery. He ended up putting two horseshoe plates on the right side of my face, miraculously saving my eye and my face. My recovery took quite a while. I ate lots of soft foods, but it was worth it. That gelding, well, he turned out great!

1 CORINTHIANS 16:13 "BE ON GUARD. STAND FIRM IN THE FAITH. BE COURAGEOUS. BE STRONG."

CHAPTER 13

THEATER

In the old west in the 1800s, the highlight was when a rolling theater troupe would come to town. My daughter, Hailey, was so involved in acting that I was at our local theater a lot. I ended up being on the board and then president of this wonderful theater group.

The theater wasn't making a lot of money, and even though it was a nonprofit, we still wanted to run it for a profit. I never understood the starving artist concept. We, as a team, worked on running it as a business with an executive director, a board of directors, staff, and all of the hundreds of volunteers.

We worked hard with a very specific focus on running this as a business with zero outside distractions, so we stayed very focused! We looked at everything from the customer's point of view, from the moment you drove into the parking lot to the back of the stage –everything was geared toward the customer experience. We put auditing procedures and budget management procedures in place. We increased the number of shows and worked to improve the customer experience by putting in better lights and sound for watching the shows, with even a red-carpet event for the first show of the run.

It took everyone working with one common goal of running a nonprofit for profit. The positive results were more employees getting to work in their chosen field, a battery of equipment, more control over our day-to-day functions, and donors knowing that we would do the right thing with their donations. Being able to manage a donor's donation in the right way would help build confidence.

This business model for the nonprofit worked. We ended up winning the Theater of the Decade award for the south region of Texas. I really appreciate all the hard work and dedication of everyone at the theater. This same concept works with other nonprofits, from horse rescues to military nonprofits. We have seen it and helped with it. Nonprofits are usually created to help, and by managing the business, you are able to do a lot better.

PROVERBS 14:23 "WORK BRINGS PROFIT BUT MERE TALK LEADS TO POVERTY."

CHAPTER 14

EAST TEXAS CONCUSSION

I was leaving West Texas with a trailer of four really good horses I had been training. I drove to Georgetown, Texas, and picked up my dad. My mom stayed to watch over the place and take care of the animals.

The total drive from my house to the coliseum in East Texas is about seven hours. We ended up driving through Davy Crockett Park in East Texas and pulled over to look at the mass of pine trees. It was midnight. There was not a truck on the road, and Davy Crocket Park smelled just like a pine air freshener.

We made it to the coliseum around two in the morning. Not many people were around, not even many horses. We unloaded our horses, dropped the trailer, and made it to the hotel.

It was a really short night, and we were back at the coliseum by 6 a.m. There was a big event that day, and the horse sale was that evening. Three of the four horses did exceptionally well during the sold-out exposition event, and the last one was also doing great for a while. When we got him in up close and in front of the crowd, the crowd stood up to clap —making a huge noise. In response, he jumped to the inside, flushed to the left, pulling me over his shoulder, and my foot got caught, and I was hanging underneath the saddle —not a good place. When I was released from the saddle, I was underneath the horse. The horse stepped on the back of my head and pushed my face into that deep sand.

I believe I was out for at least a few seconds, I knew I had a concussion. I got up and went to the gate, where somebody handed me my horse. Once I was at the gate, I just wanted to leave the arena. I thought I was just sweating a lot after the concussion. My dad noticed there was a lot of blood running down my head, down my neck into my shirt. I grabbed a handful of sand and put it on the open wound to stop the bleeding. It didn't stop it, but it did slow it down a bit.

We put up the horses and went to the hotel to clean up and rest. I know that after a concussion, you aren't supposed to sleep, so I just iced my wounds. We went back to the arena and rode four more times. It was mainly my pride that was hurt. I've done that same thing on three other horses earlier in the day –no problem. What the horse did was not his fault but completely mine. All said and done, we did pretty well, but the horses did great.

PROVERBS 3:8 "THEN YOU WILL HAVE HEALING FOR YOUR BODY AND STRENGTH FOR YOUR BONES."

CHAPTER 15

FLANK STRAP

When I was in my twenties, I needed shoulder and knee surgery. I chose to do them at the same time since they were on the same side of my body, my left. I figured I could do therapy and save a little time. It worked.

I was out riding soon as I could. However, I eventually tore up my left rotator cuff in that same shoulder. Let me explain. I was riding a young colt, and the colt fell down, and when we fell, I landed on my left shoulder.

I lived with the injury for a while, putting the left shoulder back in place whenever needed. When I finally had the surgery, the doctor prescribed lots of resting and lying around. That's not my style.

I normally sleep on the left side of the bed; however, that's the side I had the second shoulder surgery on. It was tough getting out of bed. We took a flank strap off one of the saddles, and I put it on the left side of the bed. It was a pulley system. I pulled on it, and I had freedom. I could then easily get out of bed.

Once I got better, I put the flank strap back on one of my working saddles. Kind of cool, it worked just as well-being off the saddle as it helped me get out of bed!

PSALM 146:1 "PRAISE THE LORD! LET ALL THAT I AM PRAISE THE LORD."

CHAPTER 16

MOSES

I have always taught my daughter Hailey that it's not the gentle horse that is near you that you need to look out for, but it's the horse that's behind him! Let me explain. I was feeding horses the day before we filmed our next show, the Cowboy Entrepreneur show. I had a few horses running loose in the bigger pasture, so I took the time to put them back in the barn for their dinner.

We just adopted a beautiful young Clydesdale named Moses. My wife named him that, and I felt it was appropriate for sure. While putting Moses in the stall, I forgot about one of the big ranch geldings that I had left out in the pasture. He came out of nowhere from around the side of the barn. I never saw him, and neither did Moses.

When we did see him, it was too late. That gelding was right on the back end of Moses so that Clydesdale had two options. Number one, he could face a gelding, or number two, he could run over me!

He chose to run over me not because he was an aggressive horse but because he was trying to get out of harm's way. When he did, he knocked me down so hard my head hit the barn, knocking me out.

Once I regained consciousness, I knew he had knocked me out, giving me another concussion. I iced it for most of the night and stayed awake because that's what you're supposed to do with a concussion.

The next day I'm headed to do the show, and my daughter goes with me to run the sound and one of the cameras. Hailey was on crutches, but that didn't stop her. Just like her dad, she is always game for anything. We did the show that morning, and we had a great time with our guest, Mustang Heritage Foundation.

One month later, I had the privilege to ride Heritage for three days at Will Rogers Coliseum in Fort Worth, Texas. The one thing about that show was that I couldn't put my cowboy hat on correctly. I had such a big knot on my head that it wouldn't fit right! The show was great, and the way I wore my hat made me look like a greenhorn.

JOB 9:11 "YET WHEN HE COMES NEAR, I CANNOT SEE HIM. WHEN HE MOVES BY, I DO NOT SEE HIM GO."

CHAPTER 17

ROPE 'EM IF YOU GET 'EM

I spent four days in beautiful Fort Worth, Texas. The majority of the twenty-four hours in the day were spent at Will Rogers Coliseum around fantastic mustangs and wonderful country people. I was asked to ride Heritage, the famous mascot of the Heritage Mustang Association. We were doing meet and greets, riding in the arena, and introducing thousands to the incredible iconic Mustang.

I was having so much fun, and my family and some friends were there as well, among thousands of new friends. The trainers in the competition quickly became my friends. We did some of our Cowboy Entrepreneur show from behind the stalls in the barn to give our viewers incredible access to our life.

On our way home from Fort Worth, we headed back to Fredericksburg, Texas, about a four-hour drive south. We went through a small iconic Texas town, Hico. In my rearview mirror, I could see some cows that got out of a cattle truck, so we quickly turned around and headed in that direction.

We talked to the owner of the cows, and he had a flatbed, and somehow the cows got out when he opened the back trailer door to get a tool. We immediately wanted to help, and he said, "rope 'em if you get 'em." My wife Tracy started driving our Chevy 1-Ton pick-up while my daughter Hailey was giving me a couple of ropes from underneath the backseat. We always travel with them.

I jumped in the bed of the truck, and we were in hot pursuit of cows running through this town from downtown main street to running across streets and neighborhoods. It would've been really fun, except I knew how dangerous it was for the people and the cattle. A couple of other guys jumped on their horses and drove trucks, and we went through the neighborhoods pushing the cows. We slowed down or stopped the traffic to catch them.

It was amazing teamwork. I ended up jumping in another truck while the other guys hopped in my truck. We ran several blocks on foot –whatever it took to catch these cows running through town. We eventually ended up catching them and then loading them back into his livestock trailer without any animals or people getting hurt.

It was so cool to meet and work with instant friends on a united mission, which was a high-stress situation, but we all just naturally went with our instincts of being Cowboys. After that, we went to the convenience store and grabbed a coffee, then hit the road back to the ranch.

PROVERBS 3:28 IF YOU CAN HELP YOUR NEIGHBOR NOW, DON'T SAY, "COME BACK TOMORROW, AND THEN I WILL HELP YOU."

Photographs provided by,
Anna Wiley & Claus Goldbecker, Fredericksburg, Texas

SCOTT KNUDSEN

Host of "Cowboy Entrepreneur" Television show, Keynote
Speaker, Actor, Podcast Host, Author, and Cowboy |
www.cowboyentrepreneur.com

cott Knudsen is not your ordinary fifth-gener-
ation Texas Cowboy with a business degree;
ranching is in his blood. Scott has experi-
enced all the challenging elements ranching and
being a cowboy in Texas. With all he has gone
through, his many cowboy stories overflow with
amazing life lessons, rich with wisdom. He holds
a business degree from Tarleton State University
in Stephensville, TX. He has been struck by lightning (in his head, out of his hand), played a mixed
doubles tennis tournament at the LA Forum with
Billy Jean King and Martina Navratilova for Yon-
ex, and became an award-winning national sales
representative for a Fortune 50 company. Married
with one daughter, Scott and his family live near
Fredericksburg, TX. Headquartered in Fredericksburg, Texas, at the family's Lightning K Ranch,
he owns Knudsen Equine Center, Knudsen Horses, and Knudsen Cattle Company. An American
Quarter Horse Association (AQHA) Professional
Horseman and AQHA Ambassador, he's ridden

rough stock (broncs and bulls) to racehorses, team roped, penned, and sorted. Knudsen has ridden cutting horses, worked with rescues, and trained Thoroughbreds to Morgans and Mustangs. As President of the Board for Fredericksburg Theater Company (the San Antonio area's top- rated theater company), Knudsen helped turn the non-profit's balance sheet into a $1 million-plus operation. Scott hosts the weekly "Cowboy Entrepreneur" show, which broadcasts worldwide on a dozen platforms—from iHeart to Spotify to Apple—and is featured on EQUINE NETWORK'S Horse Radio Network. Watch "Cowboy Entrepreneur" weekly on the Cowboy Entrepreneur YouTube Channel. Plus, don't miss his EQUUS Television's original series, ON THE ROAD WITH THE COWBOY ENTREPRENEUR, airing all year long. Scott will be filming an autobiography feature film called LIGHTNING K RANCH (working title), where his life story will be brought to life on the Big Screen, detailing his lightning survival story and the impact of Traumatic Brain Injury, Faith, and the power of family in this made-for-all drama by Award-Winning Producer, Rodney Stone!

In 2023, his upcoming book, "Sovereign Rein" and Scott's second book, published by Leadership

Books. Scott contributes to "Performance Horse Digest," a National Publication with over 400,000 Print and Online Subscribers. Additionally, he is an American Quarter Horse Association (AQHA) Professional Horseman and AQHA Ambassador. Scott is a Keynote Speaker and regular on the National CHRIST OVER CAREER Tour. The National Weather Service featured Knudsen in its 2020 Lightning Safety Campaign. Fox News spotlighted Knudsen's lightning survival story at the height of the lightning season. WeatherNation TV also featured Knudsen's story.

In a talk for the Texas and Southwestern Cattle Raisers Association, "When Lightning Strikes in Business and Life," Knudsen shared personal and professional obstacles he's overcome and the mindset that has helped him turn negatives into positives. He was a featured speaker and panelist at the Montana Center for Horsemanship's 2021 Horse Human and Nature Conference, a national event presented in collaboration with the University of Montana Western. Scott has also been featured in other global media companies such as The Guardian, BBC network, Fox News, America's Voice, and Weather Channel. Knudsen is now in discussions with several other feature films and television shows to continue his acting career and to host several television shows about the western industry that Scott loves so much.

www.cowboyentrepreneur.com

Photographs provided by,
Anna Wiley & Claus Goldbecker, Fredericksburg, Texas

ANNA C. WILEY AND CLAUS R. GOLDBECKER

nna Wiley's original home was Lawrence, Kansas, home of the Kansas Jayhawkers. Her early years were learning experiences in Studio, Wedding, Natural Light Family Portraits and Retinal Photography.

Claus Goldbecker came to this country from Germany with Carl Zeiss Company's Medical Division. He eventually created his own company Designing and Manufacturing Specialized Medical Equipment, Microscopes and Scientific Instruments.

Anna and Claus met through the medical community and now live in Fredericksburg, Texas. They paired up during retirement for fun photography for a few family weddings and now their special neighbors, Scott and Tracy Knudsen.

Photographs provided by,
Payton Knudsen, Georgetown, Tx

PAYTON KNUDSEN
GEORGETOWN, TEXAS

owdy, my name is Payton Knudsen. I am blessed to work full time with my husband in the cattle industry and I love what I do! Ranching is an industry in which God's creation is so evident; this is really what got me into Western Photography.

When you are surrounded by beautiful things and wonderful people every day, you feel a need to document them! You can find more photos on our website, at 16cattlecompany.com.

www.ingramcontent.com/pod-product-compliance
Lightning Source LLC
Chambersburg PA
CBHW060254030426
42335CB00014B/1685